TEACHING TIPS

Compiled
by
Jean Warren

TOTLINE PRESS
WARREN PUBLISHING HOUSE, INC.
P.O. BOX 2255
EVERETT, WA 98203

ACKNOWLEDGEMENTS

Special thanks to all the **Totline** subscribers who shared their teaching tips.

ISBN 0-911019-08-1

Edited by Elizabeth S. McKinnon
Illustrated by Paula Inmon
Cover Design by Larry Countryman
Printed in the United States of America
Printed at Snohomish Publishing Co., Inc., Snohomish, WA

CONTENTS

CLASSROOM TIPS

CURRICULUM TIPS

SPECIAL TIMES TIPS

PREFACE

The teaching tips in this book were contributed mainly by **Totline** subscribers. All ideas have been found by their authors to be inexpensive, easy and fun.

We do caution you, however, that when working with young children, it is always advisable to test new ideas before using them in the classroom.

May your life be filled with the wonder of little joys.

Jean Warren

Classroom Tips

EQUIPMENT

Classroom cubbies

- Cut down on lost mittens, toys and papers by making cubbies for your children. Purchase large cardboard shoe-storage boxes that are divided into partitions and label one partition for each child. **Joyce DeVilbiss, Silver Spring, MD**

- Or pick up used cardboard buckets at an ice cream store and cover them with Con-Tact paper. Write each child's name on his or her bucket. Some ice cream stores give away the buckets free. **Joyce DeVilbiss, Silver Spring, MD**

Individual chalkboards

- Make your own chalkboards by cutting pieces of wood or heavy cardboard into letters, numbers, animals or geometric shapes. Then paint the shapes with chalkboard paint, available at paint stores. The children can use the chalkboards for tracing, drawing, writing or for playing various games. **Betty Ruth Baker, Waco, TX**

Individual magnet boards

- Pizza pans make great individual magnet boards for learning games. **Betty Ruth Baker, Waco, TX**
- Or use metal countertop mats. **Betty Ruth Baker, Waco, TX**

Bookshelf dollhouse

- An empty shelf in a bookcase can be made into a cute dollhouse. Just attach wallpaper or giftwrap to the inside walls and glue on a fireplace, doors and windows and other decorations. Put a carpet square on the bottom of the shelf, add doll furniture and you'll be ready for "Open House!" (For a two-story house, use two shelves.)

Simple play tents

- A play tent can provide a cozy nook for quiet-time activities. Just drape a flat sheet or a blanket over a card table.
- Or slip the corners of a fitted sheet over the backs of four chairs that are of equal height.

Plastic curtain magic

- Ask parents to donate old plastic shower and window curtains. These can be used as floor coverings for water, paint and sand projects or as table coverings when painting, gluing or using clay.
  Sally J. Horton, Waukegan, IL
- The plastic curtains can also be cut into squares and used for placemats, diaper-changing mats or for outdoor seating mats. (See page 18 for using shower curtains to make art smocks.)
  Sally J. Horton, Waukegan, IL
- If you contact a local hotel, the manager may be willing to supply you with old shower curtains which can then be sterilized with a mixture of bleach and water.
  Dr. Susan A. Miller, Kutztown, PA

Hospital throw-aways

- Free for the asking are throw-away plastic containers from hospitals:

  — Large blue plastic bins that hold sterile heart-surgery instruments make excellent water-play tubs or storage boxes for oversize games and materials.

  — Smaller orange plastic containers are handy for mixing paint, holding collage materials or storing small toys.

  — Sterile water bottles with the tops cut off make paint holders that fit perfectly in the easel rack. They won't tip over when brushes are placed in them and, since the bottles are clear, young artists can see at a glance the colors they are using.
  Dr. Susan A. Miller, Kutztown, PA

Storage containers

- Small storybooks, such as Golden Books, can be stored neatly in plastic napkin holders. Check thrift stores and garage sales for bargains.
- For storing rolls of giftwrap, foil, waxed paper, etc., use extra-large soft drink cartons.
- Tiny toys will always be easy to find if you keep them stored in clear plastic shoebags.
- Cardboard pet carriers, available at veterinary clinics, are handy for storing and toting games, toys and other materials. The carriers are relatively inexpensive, and they'll last for a long time.
- Use a large detergent box to make a file box for holding professional papers — or copies of the **Totline** newsletter. Cut off the top part of the box diagonally. Then cover the bottom part of the box with colorful Con-Tact paper.

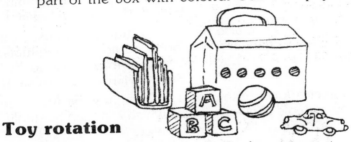

Toy rotation

- To stimulate learning, always keep some toys and learning materials in storage so that occasionally you can add something "new" to your classroom.   **Cathryn Abraham, St. Charles, IL**
- Or make a plan to rotate toys, games and other materials among the classrooms of your school.
  Cathryn Abraham, St. Charles, IL

Lost and found

- To keep the pieces of a puzzle from getting mixed up with those of other puzzles, write the name of the puzzle on the backs of all of the pieces.   **Cathryn Abraham, St. Charles, IL**
- Throughout the day, it's inevitable that odd parts of toys and games will turn up around the room. Instead of returning them to their proper places each time, make a special container just for toy and game parts. Not only will this save time, you'll always know where to look if a part is missing.

Make it last

- Preserve posters, pictures and other items you want to last from year to year by covering them with clear Con-Tact paper. The items will be easier for the children to handle, and dirt and finger marks can be wiped off easily.

  Mrs. Leslie Wagner, Chadron, NE

- Game and puzzle boxes often give out before their contents do. Solve the problem by reinforcing the boxes with masking tape on the inside corners and with Scotch tape on the outside corners before letting the children play with them.

  Cathryn Abraham, St. Charles, IL

- Spray new puzzles and gameboards with clear shellac or varnish. You'll find that they last much longer.

- Empty food boxes used for learning games will be more sturdy if you stuff them with newspaper and then tape them shut.

- Dull scissors can be frustrating for children to use. Just snip their scissors sharp by cutting through sandpaper a few times. (Note: This is not recommended for expensive shears.)

- You can bring old, hard pencil erasers back to life by rubbing them with sandpaper or with an emery board.

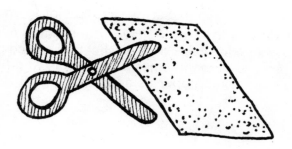

Keep it clean

- When sanitizing school furniture and fixtures with bleach and water, put the mixture into an empty window cleaner spray bottle which has been thoroughly washed and dried. The spray bottle is easy to use, and it will help prevent "dishpan hands."
  Bronwen Evans, Reading, PA

- To clean stuffed toys, rub them — or shake them in a bag — with cornmeal. Let the toys stand for a while before brushing them off.

- When game cards get sticky from too much handling, put them in a bag and shake them with talcum powder or baby powder.

- To remove felt marker ink from skin, try rubbing on toothpaste, then rinsing with water. Repeat the process until the ink disappears.

Playground equipment

- If swing seats are too slippery, cover them with a coat of paint to which you have added some fine sand. The sand will give just enough traction, and it won't scratch.

- Or cover the swing seats with pieces of foam rubber.

- To slick up a sticky slide, have your children take turns going down the slide while sitting on sheets of waxed paper. Repeat the process as many times as necessary and hand out fresh sheets of waxed paper as needed.

Personal belongings

- When working with children, it's inevitable that you will have some items you don't want them to handle. As a precautionary measure, always have at least one drawer with a childproof latch or lock.
  Cathryn Abraham, St. Charles, IL

- Stamp your own name or the name of your school in personal books. This will keep them from getting mixed up with library books.
  Cathryn Abraham, St. Charles, IL

DECORATIONS

Hang it up

- When your children paint pictures that you want to display on a wall, attach their papers to the tabletop with masking tape. The tape will keep the papers from sliding and, when the children have finished, you can unpeel the ends of the tape from the table and use them to retape the paintings to the wall. **Nancy J. Heimark, Grand Forks, ND**

- Use pull-tab rings from soft drink cans for picture hangers. Tape the bottom half of a ring to the back of a picture. Then hang the top half of the ring on a nail or hook in the wall.

- Paper clips can be used to make hooks for hanging Christmas tree decorations or paper shapes, or for constructing mobiles. Just unbend the clips to make "S" shapes.

- You can also twist pipe cleaners into "S" shapes or loops and use them for hanging lightweight items.

- Instead of using tape to hang paper shapes on a wall with a hard finish, try sticking them on with dabs of toothpaste. The shapes will look nice, and the toothpaste can be washed off the wall when you change decorations.

Bulletin board magic

- Perk up your bulletin boards by cutting borders and letters out of colorful giftwrap paper.

  Cathryn Abraham, St. Charles, IL

Bulletin board storage

- Here's a handy way to organize and store your own — or your school's — bulletin board displays. When you take down a display, put all the pieces in a small plastic trash bag. Group the small bags together by months or seasons and place them in large plastic trash bags. Use clothespins to clip the large bags on coat hangers, hang the bags on a clothes pole and put dividers between them. When it's time to change a bulletin board, you'll have a whole bagful of displays to choose from.

  Debbie Watson, Little Rock, AR

NEW STUDENTS

Easing transition

- Saying goodbye to Mom or Dad at school can be hard for a little one. Help ease a difficult separation by carrying the child over to your fish tank and letting him or her feed the fish. The physical contact, the water and the fish are all very soothing. **Kathy Rogaway, Palto Alto, CA**

- To ease the transition between home and school during the first few days of the year, place a different sticker on the floor of each child's cubby. Then give each parent several matching stickers to place, one a day, on the back of the child's hand just before coming to school. Upon arrival, the children will be eager to locate their matching stickers and will find their cubbies quickly. **Dr. Susan A. Miller, Kutztown, PA**

Labeling cubbies

- At the beginning of the school year, take a Polaroid snapshot of each child, print his or her name at the bottom and tape the picture above the child's cubby. This makes it easy for the children to locate their own cubbies and helps them learn to recognize their names. And at the end of the year, it will be fun to see how much the children have matured.
  Pat Reinik, Reading, PA

- Help younger, non-reading children locate their cubbies by themselves by placing a different picture beside each one.
  Cathryn Abraham, St. Charles, IL

Getting acquainted

- To help your children become better acquainted, substitute their names when you sing familiar songs. For example, "The Muffin Man" of Drury Lane could become Laura Karch of White Oak Street, or "Yankee Doodle" could become Michael Fisher. Using this technique gives every child a chance to be a star and shine. **Dr. Susan A. Miller, Kutztown, PA**

For parents of new students

- During the first week of school, send each parent a Sharing Time letter explaining the purposes of sharing time and giving the name of the child's assigned day to share. You might also include a few rules such as these: The child may bring one item to show to classmates; no toy weapons are allowed; the child does not have to participate in sharing if he or she chooses not to. **Nancy C. Windes, Denver, CO**

- Always make a few extra copies of such things as classroom newsletters, name-tag blanks, school supplies lists and letters to parents and put them in a New Student folder. When a new child joins your group, it will be easy to compile the information and send it home promptly.

    Nancy C. Windes, Denver, CO

HELPERS

Choosing helpers

- Classroom helpers are sure to remember their tasks if you string cleanup-job cards on loops of yarn for them to wear as necklaces. Put the cards in a basket each morning and let the children choose the necklaces they want to wear that day.
  Kathy Rogaway, Palto Alto, CA

- When choosing helpers, play a game of "Detective." First, run your "magic finger" up and down a list of your children's names. Stop at a name, then give clues such as these: "My helper is a boy. He has blonde hair. He is wearing brown pants and a green shirt. His first name begins with an 'E' and it sounds like 'eh'." Then write the initial letter of the child's name — or his or her entire name — on the board. Your children will love this game and won't realize how much they are learning while playing it.
  Maxine Pincott, Windsor, CT

- Organize your helper list by writing the first name of each child on a 3"x5" index card. Put the cards on a ring and flip them over, one at a time, when choosing classroom helpers. This way, the shy child will not be left out, and the children will learn to recognize each other's names as you read them off the cards.
  Ruth Prall, Sterling, CO

- Choose a special name, such as "Care Bears," for your group of children and use the name to design a decorative helper poster. For each child, cut a picture symbolizing your group's name from wallpaper, giftwrap or construction paper and write his or her name on it. Glue the pictures on a wall poster. Then each morning, indicate the group leader of the day by pinning a star on one of the pictures. (The leader gets first choice of where to sit at the table, helps pass the wastebasket, hand out napkins, etc.) A list of your children's names next to the poster will help you keep track of turns.
  Jane Roake, Oswego, IL

Special door helper

- To prevent a mass flow to and from your classroom, appoint a child to act as door helper. The door helper can assist in lining up the other children, counting noses and holding open all the doors.
  Maxine Pincott, Windsor, CT

PARENTS

Parent communications

- Place your Parent Bulletin Board by the entrance of your room to ensure greater visibility. **Cathryn Abraham, St. Charles, IL**

- Important notices and letters for parents often fall off cubby shelves and are lost. To solve this problem, use a shoebag to make an attractive parent "mailbox." Label each pocket with a parent's name and have mothers or fathers check daily for their "mail." **Pat Witman, Reading, PA**

- If your notices to parents regarding suitable dress for outdoor play don't seem to be getting the message across, try sharing a poem, such as the one below, with them.

> Now, when outside we do swarm,
> Make my clothes old, soft and warm.
> Soft old pants and an old hooded sweater
> So I can get dirty — what could be better?
> Comfy old sneakers, not my best pretties,
> So I can go play in the dirty old gritties.
> All my clothes will be easier to claim
> If in each thing, you please put my name.
> Spring is here — time to laugh, jump and run.
> Please won't you dress me to share in the fun?
>
> **Sally J. Horton, Waukegan, IL**

HEALTH

Toothbrush holders

- To help your children locate their own toothbrushes, put masking tape on the backs of the holders and write the children's names on the tape. After brushing, have the children dry off their toothbrushes and replace them in their holders. Check at the end of each week to see if the holders need cleaning.
  Paulette M. Skinner, Reading, PA

- For handy toothbrush holders, invert two green plastic berry baskets, one for the girls' brushes and one for the boys' brushes. The toothbrush handles will fit nicely into the spaces in the bottoms of the baskets. **Pat Reinik, Reading, PA**

Taking vitamins

- If your children are required to take vitamins at school, make a game of it by playing "Who Are You Today?" While handing out the vitamins, ask the children who they want to be — Spider-Man? Wonder Woman? Santa Claus? You'll soon find that the children can't wait to take their vitamins.
  Karen Focht, Reading, PA

Easy cold packs

- Make an easy-to-hold, dripless cold pack for bumped foreheads and cut lips by filling a vitamin bottle with water and putting it in the freezer. **Betty Silkunas, Philadelphia, PA**

- Or keep a wet sponge in the freezer to use as a cold pack. It's easier for little hands to hold than an ice cube.
  Laura Jordan, Pittsfield, MA

- A damp washcloth kept in the freezer can also be used as a cold pack.

Soap-in-a-sock

- Make sure your children always have a bar of soap available for washing hands by placing the bar in an old knee-high nylon and tying the stocking to the faucet of the sink. This will also help prevent mess. **Cathryn Abraham, St. Charles, IL**

Curriculum Tips

ART

Super smocks

- Use a tablecloth with plastic on one side and cloth on the other to make smocks for water play, painting and other messy activities. Cut the tablecloth into rectangles. Then near one end of each rectangle, cut out a circle large enough to slip over a child's head. **Kit Cooper, Pittsfield, MA**

- Make free waterproof smocks out of discarded shower curtains. Cut the curtains into child-size ovals. Then in the center of the ovals, cut out circles for head holes. **Dr. Susan A. Miller, Kutztown, PA**

- Here's another way to make smocks out of shower curtains. For each smock, cut out an 18"x36" rectangle. Fold the rectangle in half to make an 18" square and cut a head hole along the fold. Then staple the sides together, leaving room at the top for armholes. **Joyce DeVilbiss, Silver Spring, MD**

- Old pillowcases make great art smocks which can be tossed into the washing machine after each use. Cut arm and head holes along the pillowcase seams, then slip the open ends over the children's shoulders. (Use baby pillowcases for making infants' eating smocks.) **Saundra Winnett, Ft. Worth, TX**

- Discarded men's shirts worn backwards can also be used for paint smocks. Just cut off the collars and the bottom halves of the sleeves.

- For quick and easy smocks, cut arm and head holes out of plastic trash bags. These are good for extra-messy projects, since they can be thrown out after use.

Magic Markers

- Felt markers can dry out fast if their caps get lost. Solve the problem by setting the caps, open ends up, in a margarine tub or Cool Whip container filled with plaster of Paris. Make sure the plaster does not cover the holes. When the plaster dries, the markers can be put back into the caps and will stand upright until ready to be used again.

  Cynthia Holt, Danbury, CT

- Here's a way to rejuvenate your old, dry felt markers. Keep the markers stored tips down with the caps on. When the markers become dried out, remove the caps and put in a few drops of water. **Cathryn Abraham, St. Charles, IL**

- Recycle dried-out wide felt markers by letting your children dip them in paint and use them for drawing or writing.

  Barbara Jackson, Denton, TX

- Make your own Magic Markers by prying the sponge applicator tops off empty plastic shoe polish bottles, washing the tops and bottles thoroughly, then filling the bottles with watery tempera paint. **Dr. Susan A. Miller, Kutztown, PA**

- Or make pastel-colored markers by adding drops of food coloring to bottles of white shoe polish that have sponge applicator tops. **Dr. Susan A. Miller, Kutztown, PA**

- You can also make Magic Markers by using empty roll-on deodorant bottles. Just remove the rollers (they pry off easily) and wash both the rollers and the bottles. Then fill the bottles with liquid tempera paint and replace the rollers.

Tape tips

- For art projects that require using pieces of tape, cut the tape into desired lengths ahead of time. Then make tape holders for the children by lightly sticking the pieces around the edges of tuna fish cans.　**Melode Hurst, Grand Junction, CO**

- Or stick the pieces of tape along the edges of the work table.

- When art time involves using tape, children can spend more time playing with it than making things with it. Solve the problem by giving them separate pieces of tape to hold and play with in their hands.　**Melode Hurst, Grand Junction, CO**

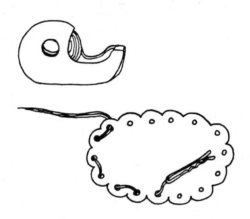

Sewing needles

- Let your children use bobby pins for sewing needles. The bobby pins are stiff, easy to thread, have blunt ends and are inexpensive. They can be used for sewing cards, for stringing beads or macaroni or for any projects that require putting string, yarn or thread through holes in paper.
  Peggy Wolf, Pittsburgh, PA

- You can also make "needles" by wrapping the ends of yarn or string with tape.

- Or dip the ends of yarn or string into glue, nail polish or melted wax and let them dry.

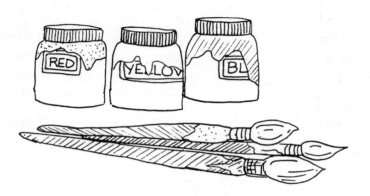

Painting tips

- To provide another dimension to your art center during the study of the five senses, add drops of food flavoring to liquid tempera paints. Put lemon flavoring in yellow paint, mint in green, vanilla in white and peppermint in red.

    Betty Ruth Baker, Waco, TX

- When painting large boxes or murals, pour some liquid detergent into the paint. This will help prevent the paint from chipping off once it has dried.

    Elisabetta DiStravolo, West Reading, PA

- Thicken easel paint and paint used for murals with liquid starch to cut down on drips.

- To make paint that will adhere to slick surfaces, such as foil, waxed paper, Styrofoam or plastic, mix dry tempera with liquid soap.

- A few drops of glycerin or oil of wintergreen added to paints will keep them fresh and sweet-smelling.

- To preserve liquid tempera paints, add a little alum.

- If you want paints to have a glossy look, mix them with condensed milk.

- Painting pre-drawn shapes can be difficult for young children. Instead, let them experiment freely with brush strokes and color-mixing on large sheets of paper. Then cut their papers into desired shapes when the paint has dried.

Paint containers

- Cupcake pans or muffin tins make excellent containers for paint projects when several different colors are needed.
  Mrs. Mame Reback, Kenmore, NY

- Egg cartons make handy paint containers when your children are painting with Q-Tips. Cut the cartons in thirds to make four-part containers and pour small amounts of paint into the cups. **Barbara H. Jackson, Denton, TX**

- Tupperware cups in 4- or 6-ounce sizes make great paint containers. They also have lids which can be resealed to keep the paint from drying out. **Vicki Shannon, Napton, MO**

- Cut down on paint drips by storing liquid tempera in glue bottles. Any amount of paint can then be squirted quickly and neatly into paint pans. **Jane Roake, Oswego, IL**

- The glue bottles also make for less messy dribble painting. Just open the screw-on caps partway and let the children dribble the paint onto paper. **Jane Roake, Oswego, IL**

- Store your liquid tempera paints in dishwashing liquid bottles. The paint can then be squirted into paint dishes or cups, even by the children. **Mrs. Leslie Wagner, Chadron, NE**

- Put liquid tempera into Worcestershire sauce bottles and let your children use them for drip painting.

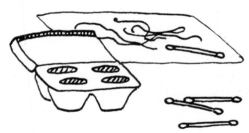

Easel paint containers

- Cut egg cartons into sections to use as paint containers at the easel. **Cathryn Abraham, St. Charles, IL**

- Or use baby food jars, if you want containers that have lids.
  Cathryn Abraham, St. Charles, IL

- Commercial cake frosting containers make good paint holders for the easel and, between art times, their lids will prevent the paint from drying out.
  Elisabetta DiStravolo, West Reading, PA

Paint container holders

- When using baby food jars as paint containers, make a holder for them by cutting circles out of the lid of an egg carton.
  Barbara H. Jackson, Denton, TX
- Or put the baby food jars in an empty soft drink carton, which you can also use as a tote.
- To prevent paint cups from tipping over when children are painting with brushes, make a cup holder from an empty milk or juice carton. Cut holes along the length of the carton and pop in the paint cups. **Barbara Kingsley, Flushing, NY**
- To keep paint jars from tipping over while being used on the art table, make holders out of sponges. Cut holes the exact size of the jars in the center of the sponges, then fit the jars in the holes. Besides keeping the paint jars upright, the sponges will also catch drips. **Jean L. Woods, Tulsa, OK**
- Use small peanut butter jars for paint containers. They have wide mouths and won't tip over when inserted in a plastic utility tote. Use the tote when painting at tables or on the floor.
  Ruth Engle, Kirkland, WA

Painting handles

- To keep tiny hands clean when painting with cotton balls, try this. Clip spring-type clothespins to the cotton balls and let the children use the clothespins as handles.
  Gina Masci, Arlington, MA
- Clothespin handles also work well when painting with small sponge pieces. **Kathy Sizer, Tustin, CA**
- Or use clothespins clipped to small squares of felt to make paintbrushes.

Paint cleanup

- Adding a small amount of liquid dishwashing detergent to tempera paint will make drips and spills easier to wipe up. It will also help in washing paint out of children's (and teachers') clothing.
  Carol J. Luckenbill, Bernville, PA
  Cathryn Abraham, St. Charles, IL
  Judy Laureano, Reading, PA

- To extend paint and to make it easier to wash out of clothing, add a little powdered detergent to the dry tempera as you mix it with water. Make sure to use a brand that is nontoxic, especially when working with very young children.
  Lynn Meyers, Pittsfield, MA

Homemade watercolors

- Here's an inexpensive way to make your own watercolor sets. Pour different colors of leftover tempera paint into egg carton cups and set them aside to dry and harden. Then use the paints with water and brushes, just as you would ordinary watercolors.

Spatter painting

- Round spatter screens that are placed over frying pans to keep grease off stoves can be used with toothbrushes for spatter painting. Look for the screens in the kitchenware departments of large stores.

Sponge printing and painting

- Use foam rubber Lauri Picture Puzzle pieces for sponge printing. Let your children dip the pieces in paint and then press them on paper.
  Sr. Mary Bezold, Melbourne, KY

- Foam rubber brushes, available at paint stores, are great for sponge-painting projects. The brushes come in various sizes and are relatively inexpensive.

Fingerpainting fun

- To keep paint contained in a desired area when fingerpainting directly on a table, make a "fence" on the tabletop with masking tape. **Lanette L. Gutierrez, Olympia, WA**
- Very young children can enjoy fingerpainting while sitting in high chairs. There's no need for paper — the children can paint directly on the high chair trays. Painting with pudding is a real favorite. **Marcia Berquist, Virginia, MN**

Fingerpaints

- Besides instant pudding, some other edibles that children can use for fingerpaints are whipped cream and yogurt. **Melode Hurst, Grand Junction, CO**
- For non-edible fingerpaints, try liquid starch or soap powder whipped with water. **Melode Hurst, Grand Junction, CO**
- Spray scented shaving cream all over a large table and let the children fingerpaint with it. This not only helps develop sense perception, it also cleans the tabletop beautifully. **Debbie Sipola, Hales Corners, WI**
- Make fingerpainting with shaving cream more interesting by adding a dash of tempera paint or a few drops of food coloring. **Betty Ruth Baker, Waco, TX**
- To make an easy, economical fingerpaint, mix until smooth 2 tablespoons cornstarch and 2 tablespoons cold water. Add 1 cup boiling water and stir until smooth again. For color, add dry tempera or food coloring to the mixture. **Agnes Kirchgasler, Salt Lake City, UT**

Fingerpaint paper

- Freezer wrap — the kind with one waxed side — is great for fingerpainting and other types of painting projects. The freezer wrap, which comes in large rolls, won't tear when wet and is relatively inexpensive.　**Melode Hurst, Grand Junction, CO**

- When your supply of fingerpaint paper runs out, glossy gift-wrap paper, either new or used, makes a good substitute.
  Betty Ruth Baker, Waco, TX

Fingerpaint prints

- To eliminate torn papers and to facilitate cleanup when finger-painting, let your children make mono-prints. Have the children fingerpaint designs directly on plastic trays. When each child finishes, lay a piece of construction paper on top of his or her design and rub across the back of the paper with your hand. Lift the paper from the tray, and the child will have a lovely print to take home. Following the activity, the trays can easily be rinsed off in the sink.
  Dr. Susan A. Miller, Kutztown, PA

Easy paper chains

- When your children are first learning how to make paper chains, let them use strips cut from colorful pages of glossy magazines. The slick paper is easier to paste than construction paper.　**Jean L. Woods, Tulsa, OK**

Glue tips

- To help children apply glue easily and uniformly, have them use Q-Tips for gluing small items and small foam rubber brushes, available at paint stores, for gluing larger ones.
  Karen Seehusen, Ft. Dodge, IA

- When making paper mosaics, let very young children use cold cream, petroleum jelly or other thick, nontoxic ointments as glue substitutes. **Melode Hurst, Grand Junction, CO**

- To prevent the caps of glue containers (or paint jar lids) from sticking shut, wipe a thick coat of petroleum jelly on the threads of the caps the first time the containers are opened.
  Dr. Susan A. Miller, Kutztown, PA

- Paste won't dry out as fast if you keep a damp piece of sponge in the jar.

Glue containers

- Have each child bring an 8-ounce bottle of glue to keep at school as part of his or her school supplies. Then transfer the glue into 1¼-ounce bottles for the children to use during art activities. The small bottles are easy for the children to handle and can be refilled throughout the school year.
  Nancy C. Windes, Denver, CO

- For small craft projects, use milk gallon lids as glue containers. The children won't stick their whole hands in the containers, and there is less mess to clean up afterwards.
  Elisabetta DiStravolo, West Reading, PA

- Disposable communion cups make great individual glue containers. They hold just the right amount of glue, so there is little waste, and using the small cups aids in developing fine motor coordination. **Betty Turman, Reading, PA**

- Use margarine tubs for glue or paste containers. Their lids make for easy cleanup and storage.
  Cathryn Abraham, St. Charles, IL

Playdough tips

- For a fun addition to your study of the five senses, work a drop of food flavoring and a drop of food coloring into homemade playdough. Match scents with colors, such as mint flavoring with green and lemon flavoring with yellow.

  Betty Ruth Baker, Waco, TX

- It won't matter if your children put their art masterpieces in their mouths if you let them use pie dough or thawed bread dough as playdough substitutes.

  Melode Hurst, Grand Junction, CO

- Or let them use a tasty mixture of peanut butter and powdered milk as playdough. **Melode Hurst, Grand Junction, CO**

- To make playdough easier to handle, try adding a little vegetable oil.

- A small amount of alum added to playdough will keep it from molding.

- Work a few drops of oil of peppermint into playdough to keep it fresh.

- Keep playdough soft by storing it in an airtight container with a piece of damp cloth.

- For an easy homemade playdough, mix together 1 cup flour, 1/2 cup salt, 3 to 4 tablespoons water, 1 tablespoon vegetable oil and a few drops of food coloring.

  Mrs. David Zucker, Reno, NV

Crayons

- Store crayons in wide-mouth containers according to colors — all yellow crayons in one container, all red crayons in another container, etc. Then use the containers for color-matching games when your children are putting crayons away after art projects.

- New crayons won't break as easily if you wrap them with masking tape before letting the children use them.

No more chalk smears

- Children love to color with chalk, but their pictures can be ruined if the chalk smears. Protect your children's creations by coating them lightly with hair spray.

Cathryn Abraham, St. Charles, IL

Printing with stamps

- Invest in an assortment of rubber stamps in animal, flower or toy shapes. Your children can use them year after year for making giftwrap paper, greeting cards, cards for matching games or for stamping designs on watercolor paintings.

- Rubber stamps don't have to be fancy to be fun to use. Ask businesses to donate old or outdated office stamps they may have on hand. "Air Mail" stamps might be one example.

Print remover

- Use rubbing alcohol to remove print from plastic egg cartons and margarine tub lids.

- Or, if rubbing alcohol doesn't work, try nail polish remover.

Dyeing tips

- When dyeing macaroni by shaking it in a plastic bag with food coloring, add a few drops of rubbing alcohol instead of water. The alcohol produces brilliant colors and helps the macaroni dry quickly. And it won't make the macaroni sticky the way water does. **Dr. Susan A. Miller, Kutztown, PA**

- Instead of using commercial Easter egg dyes, try boiling eggs with the following natural ingredients: beets for red; cranberry juice for pink; onion skins for yellow; spinach for green; coffee or tea for brown; blueberries for blue.

Pretty picture frames

- Cut the tops off decorative facial tissue boxes and save them to use as picture frames. Glue paper on the backs of the boxtops, turn them over and let the children draw or paint inside the frames. **Fannie Blackledge, Heath, OH**

- Or use the boxtops to frame favorite pictures the children have already made. **Fannie Blackledge, Heath, OH**

- You can also make cute picture frames by gluing popsicle sticks or tongue depressors together in square shapes for your children to decorate.

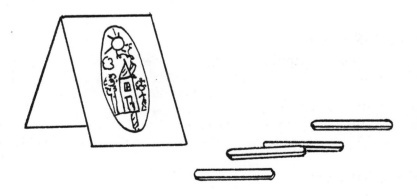

Time-saver

- Make paper shapes or patterns for your children in a jiffy by always cutting out four, six or eight at a time.

  Cathryn Abraham, St. Charles, IL

Glitter bottles

- For neat glitter dispensers, use plastic bottles with perforated caps, such as food seasoning bottles or bottles that cookie sprinkles come in. When your children use the bottles for art projects, their hands will stay cleaner, and less glitter will be wasted.

  Nancy C. Windes, Denver, CO

Holiday hats

- Purchase a supply of white paper hats — the kind restaurant workers wear — through a restaurant supply house (or check with a restaurant manager to find out where you can purchase them locally). Then throughout the year, let your children decorate the hats for holidays and wear them in marching band parades.

  Judith Lahore, Seattle, WA

Gift planters

- Half-pint milk cartons filled with potting soil and planted two weeks in advance with marigold or other fast-growing seeds make beautiful planters for children to take home as gifts. As a finishing touch, punch holes in the sides of the cartons and tie with colorful yarn.

  Betty Turman, Reading, PA

Greeting card tips

- For some children, making two Mother's Day or Father's Day cards can alleviate hurt feelings and confusion.

  Cathryn Abraham, St. Charles, IL

- Here's a fun tip for Valentine's Day. After your children make valentines for their families, put their cards in addressed, stamped envelopes. Then place all the cards in one large envelope and mail it to: Postmaster, Loveland, Colorado 80537. If your valentines arrive in Loveland by February 6th, they will be remailed with a Loveland postmark and arrive in time for Valentine's Day.   **Ellen Javernick, Loveland, CO**

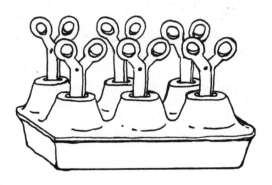

Storage tips

- To store children's scissors neatly, turn an egg carton upside down and make a hole in each of the 12 bumps. Then stick the scissors, blade ends down, into the holes.

  Lynn Meyers, Pittsfield, MA

- To keep construction paper sorted by colors and easily accessible, store it in stacked in-out baskets — the kind used on desktops and available at stationery stores.

  Pat Witman, Reading, PA

- A cheaper but less sturdy alternative would be to use a stack of gift boxes with the ends cut out.

  Pat Witman, Reading, PA

- Store yarn in liquor store boxes which are divided into partitions. The boxes are often given away free.

- Or put balls of yarn in a net onion bag and pull the ends of the yarn out through the holes as you need it.

Cleanup tips

- Using common household disposables during art time will make cleanup easier. Plastic meat trays, aluminum pie tins and frozen food trays are excellent for holding paint or glue for table activities, and yogurt containers make handy paint holders for the easel. Use the lids as covers for the paint holders or as individual paste containers. At the conclusion of art time, just throw out the disposables, perhaps saving the pie tins for recycling. **Maxine Pincott, Windsor, CT**

- An old plastic tablecloth covering the work area makes cleanup easier after art projects that require paint, sand, glitter or water. Just shake out the cloth, or wipe it clean with a damp sponge. A tablecloth with a non-stick backing works best.
  Nancy C. Windes, Denver, CO

- Use an old shower curtain or an outdoor grass carpet under your work table to catch spills during messy art projects.
  Lanette L. Gutierrez, Olympia, WA

- Before art time, fold over the top edges of a large paper bag, then tape the bag to one end of your work table. When the children have finished their art projects, scraps can easily be swept off the table into the bag.

MUSIC

Favorite songs

- Keep on hand a list of the songs you have taught your children. They really enjoy singing old favorites, and it's easy to forget which songs they know. The list will also be useful if you ever have to have a substitute teacher.

  Ellen Javernick, Loveland, CO

- "The Wheels on the Bus" is a perennial favorite, but sometimes the bouncing up and down can get a bit out of hand. To combat this and to encourage the use of seat belts, have the children pretend to "buckle-up" before they begin singing. No longer will you have bodies bouncing out of chairs!

  Ellen Javernick, Loveland, CO

Music and stories

- Before telling children the story of a musical classic such as "Peter and the Wolf," follow the Suzuki method of letting them listen to the piece as background music for several weeks. When you tell the story, the children already will have learned to distinguish the various melodies and to anticipate what comes next. Follow up with another few weeks of listening, and the children will never forget the music they learned.

  Ellen Javernick, Loveland, CO

- While playing music, tell stop-and-start stories about characters who wake up, dance around, then fall asleep again. Examples would be dolls that come alive at night in a toy shop, then quickly fall asleep when the shopkeeper returns, or jelly beans that roll around in their jar when the cupboard is closed, then stop when the cupboard is opened. Vary the volume and tempo of the music to match the characters' actions.

  Ellen Javernick, Loveland, CO

Music and art

- Let children paint watercolor washes as they listen to music. Then cut their paintings into giant musical notes and mount them on a bulletin board with the title, "Music in the Air."

  Ellen Javernick, Loveland, CO

Playing instruments

- If your children tend to start playing their musical instruments before the record starts for their marching band, talk with them about how it would sound if the musicians on the record all started playing at different times — not very nice! A simple affirmation such as, "We want our music to sound pretty, so we all start playing our instruments when the record begins," will help even very young children wait until the music starts.

  Yosie Yoshimura, Gardena, CA

- To develop auditory discrimination, tape a piece of music, occasionally changing the volume from loud to soft. Then have the children accompany the music with rhythm instruments and adjust their playing whenever they hear a volume change on the tape.

  Ellen Javernick, Loveland, CO

- Your music units will come alive if you invite several adults to visit your class and demonstrate various instruments. If possible, arrange to keep a few instruments on loan so your children can experiment with producing sounds themselves.

  Karen Seehusen, Ft. Dodge, IA

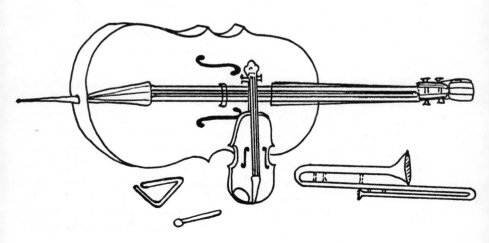

Music with maracas

- Fill plastic egg-shaped pantyhose containers with buttons or dried beans, tape the halves together and let your children use them as maracas, shaking them as they listen or dance to music. **Suzanne L. Friedrich, Pittsburgh, PA**

- To add a new sound to your rhythm band, let tiny hands shake vitamin bottles that have been partly filled with salt, rice, pebbles, nuts or screws. Seal bottles that do not have childproof lids with cloth tape. **Betty Silkunas, Philadelphia, PA**

Musical hugs

- Instead of "Musical Chairs," play "Musical Hugs." Clear a large space in the room for the children to move about while listening to music. When the music stops, have everyone hug someone nearby. If several children are close together, they can have a group hug. **Ellen Javernick, Loveland, CO**

If you don't play an instrument

- Ask a friend who plays the piano or guitar to record the music of your children's favorite songs on tape.

GENERAL LEARNING

Flannelboard tips

- If your classroom has a storage container on wheels, you can use it as a flannelboard as well as a room divider. Just attach flannel securely to the back with a staple gun.
  Karen Seehusen, Ft. Dodge, IA

- For easy-to-store flannelboards, purchase old fold-up gameboards at garage sales and cover them with flannel. The boards are sturdy and will stand up by themselves. Make several different backgrounds and have them ready to use for favorite stories and activities. **Ruth Prall, Sterling, CO**

- You can even cut holes in one of the boards and use it with finger puppets. **Ruth Prall, Sterling, CO**

- A carpet sample — or a piece of indoor-outdoor carpeting — can be used as a flannelboard. Both are available at carpet stores and are relatively inexpensive.

- When making a flannelboard, slip a piece of wire screen between the flannel and the backing and you'll be able to use it with magnets.

Flannelboard shapes

- Create flannelboard shapes easily and inexpensively by making them out of paper towels. Thick, white, rather spongy towels work best. You can use felt markers to decorate the shapes, and the children will love playing with them.
  Karen Focht, Reading, PA

- Save sponge-type fabric softener sheets after taking them out of the dryer. They can be cut into pieces and used as backing for paper flannelboard shapes.

- Other materials that can be used for flannelboard shapes or for backing are felt, flannel, flocked wallpaper, sandpaper and fabric interfacing.

Learning the ABC's

- Help your children learn to recognize the letters of the alphabet by giving them each a 26-page scrapbook to use as an "Alphabet Book." Each time they learn a new letter, have them glue a small and a capital version of the letter in their books along with items or pictures of things whose names begin with the letter. For example, their "B" page might contain a bear cut from fuzzy material, a deflated balloon, a picture of a boat they have colored and cut out and a sticker with a ball on it. Your children are sure to be very proud of their finished books!
  Mrs. Leslie Wagner, Chadron, NE

- When introducing a new letter of the alphabet, make a special container for the children to fill with items that begin with that letter. For example, put "H" items in a "Hocus-Pocus Hat," or "J" items in a pair of jeans with the legs stitched or tied closed at the bottoms. **Karen Seehusen, Ft. Dodge, IA**

Teaching left from right

- To help your children make sure they are putting their shoes on the right feet, mark the inside arches of their shoes with red arrows that point towards each other when the shoes are in the correct positions. **Cathryn Abraham, St. Charles, IL**

- To help your children learn to distinguish their right hands from their left, introduce a hand puppet with a name such as "Happy," and have him shake hands with each child at the beginning of the day. Whenever necessary, a reminder to "use the hand you use to shake hands with Happy" will help even very young children remember which hand is their right one.
  Yosie Yoshimura, Gardena, CA

- Or have your children hold up their hands with their fingers together and their thumbs outstretched. The forefinger and thumb of their left hand will form the letter "L."

Play props

- When making play telephones for your children, use string and cottage cheese cartons rather than string and paper cups. The cottage cheese cartons give a clearer sound.

  Judith Lahore, Seattle, WA

- Make inexpensive props for the housekeeping corner by gluing pictures of foods that illustrate well-balanced breakfasts, lunches and dinners on paper plates. Cover the plates with clear Con-Tact paper to make them last longer.

  Carol W. Adams, Clinton, MD

- To make a mask that won't interfere with a child's seeing or breathing, cut out the mask face and attach it to a paper headband that fits around the child's forehead. Make sure that the chin of the mask face is above the child's eyes.

Puppet tips

- Thick, spongy paper towels can be cut out and sewn into mitten shapes for hand puppets. Slip cardboard inside the mittens before decorating them with felt markers so the ink won't soak through.

- Don't throw out those stray gloves! Cut off the fingers and use them for finger puppets. Draw features on rubber glove fingers with permanent marking pens.

Puzzle tips

- Here's a great way to make use of those stray puzzle pieces that always seem to accumulate. Place all the puzzle pieces on a large sheet of white paper. Then trace around each puzzle piece, copy the designs and fill in the colors with felt markers. Laminate the paper and put the puzzle pieces in a Ziploc bag. Your children can then use the paper as a gameboard and place the puzzle pieces on their matching shapes. **Debbie Jones, Las Vegas, NV**

- Save picture postcards you get in the mail and use them to make puzzles. Just snip the postcards into desired shapes and store the pieces in separate envelopes.

- Check garage sales for torn or tattered storybooks that are beyond repair. You can cut out the pictures and use them to make puzzles.

- When making puzzles, cut pictures to fit inside Styrofoam meat trays. Your children can then use the trays as holders when putting the puzzles together.

Learning games

- Children get restless during group learning times if they have to sit and listen for too long. Instead of having your children name shapes, numbers, etc. that you hold up, tape the objects to be learned to the wall and have each child get up and point to one you name. This gives the child something to do, and the others will watch like hawks to see if their friend makes a mistake. **Sally J. Horton, Waukegan, IL**

- Playing a game of "Memory" will help children of all ages to learn colors, shapes, numbers, letters, words and names. For each game, use 10 or 12 index cards and make two cards for each color, shape, number or whatever you want to teach. Place the cards face down on a table. Then have the players name each color, shape or number as they turn the cards face up. **Peggy Klasse, Westbrook, MN**

Learning-game materials

- Save your magnetic memo holders and add to your collection. The holders can be used with your magnet board for sorting and classifying games, for likeness and difference games and for counting and matching.

  Betty Ruth Baker, Waco, TX

- When playing classification games, egg cartons make excellent trays for sorting buttons, dried beans and peas and various pasta shapes. **Betty Ruth Baker, Waco, TX**

- To make cards for number-matching games — or faces on paper-plate clocks — cut numbers out of old calendars.

- Use paint chips and paint sample cards from paint stores for color-matching games.

- Use the following materials for matching and classification games: labels from canned goods; brand names and logos cut from food boxes; picture postcards; matchbook covers (with matches removed); colorful brochures (check travel agencies).

- To make quick and easy beanbags, fill old mittens with dried beans or rice and sew the wrists closed with heavy yarn or thread.

- Check thrift stores for old breadboxes. They make great "garages" for toy cars and trucks.

41

Sandbox fun

- Use any of the following sand substitutes when making a sandbox: cornmeal, crumbled cork, washed coffee grounds, dried beans or peas, rice, Styrofoam pieces, dry cereals, salt.

- Inexpensive funnels for sand play can be made by cutting off the top halves of plastic dishwashing liquid bottles.

Water play

- Straws are great to use for blowing bubbles during water play. To prevent the children from sucking up the soapy water by mistake, poke holes near the tops of the straws first.
  Jenifer Contaya, Arlington, TX

- Make soap bubbles last longer by adding a few tablespoons of sugar to the soapy water.   **Jenifer Contaya, Arlington, TX**

- Or try this mixture: 2 quarts water, 1/4 cup glycerin and 3/4 cup liquid soap.

- For fun bubble-makers, let your children use plastic six-pack holders. Have them dip the holders in soapy water and then wave them in the air.

Sensory learning

- Children love playing with shiny objects that reflect a distorted image. Set up a Looking Corner and stock it with such things as aluminum foil, foil wallpaper, shiny hubcaps and perhaps an old chrome coffee pot or toaster.

- Use plastic food seasoning bottles with perforated caps to make containers for sniffing and smelling. Just glue small circles cut from an old nylon stocking on the undersides of the caps.

Special Times Tips

TRANSITION TIMES

Getting attention

- Establish a "lights-out" signal by turning off your room lights whenever you want your children to stop what they are doing and listen. Use the signal for announcing cleanup time, asking for quiet voices or for inviting small groups to join you for activities.   **Nancy C. Windes, Denver, CO**

- When you want your children to stop what they are doing and gather in a special area of the room, roll a large ball to a child who is already there. Have the child call out his or her name and then roll the ball back to you. When the other children see and hear this signal, they will respond quickly in order to get their turns, too.
  Nancy Hartman, Fleetwood, PA

- Try whispering instead of speaking in a loud voice when you want to get your children's attention. They'll usually quiet down fast in case they might be missing something!

Changing the pace

- To help your children quiet down between activities, clap a rhythm for them to copy. Start by clapping loud, then gradually clap softer until finally, your hands are resting in your lap.
  Betty Ruth Baker, Waco, TX

- A fun way to make use of transition time is to play guessing games. Give clues such as these: "I am thinking of a girl who is wearing a red shirt and blue pants. I am thinking of a boy who is sitting next to Michael. I am thinking of a girl whose first name begins with 'S.' I am thinking of a boy who has a sister named Amanda."   **Barbara Kingsley, Flushing, NY**

- When your children need a minute or two to settle down after an active time, have them sit quietly and close their eyes. Then tell them that together you are going to slowly count to 10, 20 or 30. Not only will the children get a little rest, they'll also be learning how to count. And they'll like knowing exactly when the quiet time will be over. **Peggy Wolf, Pittsburgh, PA**

Moving around

- For transition time, invite your children to put on their coats and come sit outside for "nibbles." Serve a simple snack, such as peanut butter and cracker sandwiches. Let this be a free-choice activity, allowing the children to leave as soon as they have finished chewing. **Kathy Rogaway, Palo Alto, CA**

- To make lining up more fun and to enhance motor skills, make a balance-beam "bridge" for your children to cross. Cut two 5"-wide strips from a carpet sample and tape them together end to end with duct tape. Place the "bridge" on the floor alongside a smiling paper alligator and have the children walk across it, being careful not to let the alligator "nip" their toes. **Cindy Kostoff, Findlay, OH**

- Following snack time, put crumbs in a cup and take your children outside to feed the birds. This is a great transition activity, and you'll be recycling the crumbs, too. **Kathy Rogaway, Palo Alto, CA**

Let's pretend

- Here are some fun things for your children to do at transition times:
  - Pretend to be a bowl of Jello and shake all over.
  - Pretend to lock lips and put the key in a pocket.
  - Pretend to put on magic ears for listening.
  - Pretend to walk in tiptoe boots, Indian moccasins or Santa's-Elf shoes. **Betty Ruth Baker, Waco, TX**

QUIET TIMES

Nap time

- As a quick reward for those who sleep or rest quietly during nap time, make nap-time necklaces. Cut out 2"x2" paper shapes, such as Christmas trees or hearts, punch holes in the tops and string them on loops of yarn. On each shape write a child's name along with a message such as, "Julie took a great nap," or "Dan took a super-duper rest." Then decorate the shape with a colorful sticker, a rubber stamp design or a happy face drawing. Not only will the necklaces serve as good incentives, they will also let parents know that their children have had naps. **Jane Roake, Oswego, IL**

- If children are having difficulty settling down at nap time, put small drops of cologne on the backs of their hands for them to sniff. The deep breathing will help them relax. **Jean L. Woods, Tulsa, OK**

Quiet-time activities

- For a quiet-down activity, try "Blanket Toy Time." Fill coffee cans or dishpans with small toys that are different from those in general use and place a receiving blanket or similar-size piece of cloth on top of each container. When a quiet time is needed, let each child choose a container, spread out the blanket and play on the blanket with just those toys found in the container. Since the toys are special and the children don't have to share, "Blanket Toy Time" provides a welcome relief from the usual classroom routine. **Sally J. Horton, Waukegan, IL**

- To help your children calm down in the midst of a hectic day, put on some soothing recorded music and let them draw or paint while they listen. This is an especially good activity to use during the busy holiday season.

OUTDOOR TIMES

Field trips

- To help keep track of your children on field trips, arrange to have them dress in matching T-shirts or matching colors.
  Cathryn Abraham, St. Charles, IL

- If you're taking a field trip to a place where there will be lots of other people, plan to carry a helium-filled balloon or wear a brightly colored scarf on your head so your children can easily spot you in the crowd.   **Joyce Warden, Philadelphia, PA**

- When going on field trips, have each child wear a name tag with your school's name, address and telephone number on it.   **Cathryn Abraham, St. Charles, IL**

- For quick and easy cleanups, take along some diaper wipes when going on field trips.   **Cathryn Abraham, St. Charles, IL**

- If you're going on a field trip by car, guard against hurt fingers by having the children put their hands on top of their heads before you close the car doors.

- Don't forget to take a camera and a tape recorder when you go on field trips. Later, the photos and recorded tapes will provide a good review of what your children learned.

Short walks

- To discourage stragglers when taking a walk, make a "train" by stringing large wooden beads on a length of clothesline, spacing them apart and knotting the rope before and after each bead. The children can each hold onto a bead and take turns being the "engine" and the "caboose."

  Cindy Kostoff, Findlay, OH

- Wearable snacks are great for walks and nature hikes. String Cheerios on yarn to make edible necklaces.

- Or core apples and string them on ribbons for the children to wear around their necks.

- When going on nature walks, give each child an empty egg carton in which to put found treasures.

- Or put a band of masking tape, sticky side out, around each child's wrist for holding leaves, seeds and other small, lightweight items.

Nature-walk take-alongs

- A shopping bag for holding miscellaneous items. (A shoebox in the bottom will make the bag sturdier.)

- A large magnifying glass for observing nature up close.

- A bottle of hair spray for spritzing delicate weeds and fluffy seed pods which the children collect.

Outdoor clothing

- To cut down on the number of lost mittens, try safety-pinning or clipping them to the cuffs of the children's jackets.
  Cathryn Abraham, St. Charles, IL

- Here's a nifty way to make use of old legwarmers. When dressing children to play in the snow, slip the legwarmers over their arms after putting on their snowsuits and mittens. The legwarmers will prevent snow from getting between their mittens and their sleeves, keeping their wrists warm and toasty.
  Kim and Sheryl Davids, Buffalo Center, IA

- When boots just don't seem to want to go on over a child's shoes, put plastic bags over his or her shoes first, and the boots should slip on easily.

- Have your children start at the bottom when buttoning up their coats or jackets. They'll be more likely to get all the buttons in the right buttonholes.

- When zippers stick, don't despair! Just rub them with a lead pencil to get them gliding smoothly again.

Outdoor fun

- What could be more fun on a sunny day than an outdoor art show? In addition to displaying the children's work on walls and portable easels, include some of these ideas: pictures drawn with colored chalk on the sidewalk; colorful string or yarn woven in a fence; large sculptures created with giant discards; pictures hung from a line with clothespins.

  Ellen Javernick, Loveland, CO

- Here's another fun activity for a sunny day. Provide your children with large paintbrushes and buckets of water and let them "paint" walls, fences and other outdoor surfaces.

- Or assemble outdoor riding toys and let your children have a "car wash."

- Children love talking through megaphones. Make several for them to use outdoors by cutting the top halves off of empty bleach bottles. (The megaphones can also be used when you're teaching a unit on sounds.)

Sandboxes

- Even if your outdoor area is small, or cats live in your neighborhood, your children can still enjoy a sandbox. Fill a baby bathtub with sand and set it outside on a small table. The sand can be used either dry or wet, and the tub can be stored indoors when not in use.

  Ellen Javernick, Loveland, CO

- Use an old automobile tire to make mini-sandboxes for your play area. Lay the tire flat and cut it in half horizontally to make two rounds. Then fill the rounds with sand.

Riding toys

- For a realistic gas-pump hose to use with outdoor riding toys, fit an old garden hose with a pistol-grip nozzle. The nozzles are available at hardware stores.

  Karen Seehusen, Ft. Dodge, IA

- Make "drivers' licenses" and string them on loops of yarn for your children to wear while playing with riding toys. They'll be more likely to follow safety rules if they know that their licenses can be suspended for "reckless driving."

Ending outdoor time

- When it's time to stop playing and come indoors, these two signals will help get the children's attention. First, raise one hand as a sign to line up. Then, with the children who are first to form a line, start counting, saying the alphabet or naming the months of the year together. Hearing this second signal, the others will quickly join in line to help with the counting or naming.

  Nancy C. Windes, Denver, CO

SNACK TIMES

Table tips

- For special days, provide centerpieces for the snack tables. Let the children share in making the centerpieces — or make them yourself as a surprise from the teacher.
  Betty Ruth Baker, Waco, TX

- To help children with name recognition and to encourage them to make new friends, make place cards for them to set on the table at snack time. **Betty Ruth Baker, Waco, TX**

- Or write the names of the children on paper cups and use the cups as place cards.

Placemats

- Let each child design his or her own placemat to use on the table at snack time. **Betty Ruth Baker, Waco, TX**

- To help children learn how to set a table, make plastic-covered placemats with cutouts of knives, forks, spoons, cups, plates and napkins glued in their proper places.
  Linnae Newman, Reading, PA

- Make washable placemats out of vinyl window shades. On each mat, use a permanent felt marker to draw a large circle for a plate and a small circle for a cup in their proper places. Then at the top, label each mat by writing "Steven's Place," "Jennifer's Place," etc. **Joyce DeVilbiss, Silver Spring, MD**

- Here's another way to make personalized placemats. For each child, cut an oval shape out of heavy paper and, in the center, glue a snapshot of the child, brought from home. Write the child's name under the picture, let him or her decorate the rest of the mat, then laminate the placemat or cover it with clear Con-Tact paper. **Erma Hunt, Winston-Salem, NC**

- Have your children decorate placemats for each season. Use a design such as a tree in spring, summer, fall and winter. All four placemats can be sent home at the end of the year.
  Erma Hunt, Winston-Salem, NC

- For each child, make a different colored or patterned placemat and cut off one of the corners. Then at snack time, let your children find their places by matching the corners with the corresponding placemats.

Just-for-fun tips

- Make napkin rings by cutting cardboard tubes into sections and covering them with giftwrap paper or foil.

- Make ice cubes with juice and put a small piece of fruit in each one.

- Stick straws through colorful paper shapes for use at holiday times.

Pouring and passing tips

- Your children are likely to drink more milk if they are allowed to pour it themselves. For a pitcher, let them use a clear plastic 8-ounce measuring cup to which a small amount of milk has been added.   **Kathy Rogaway, Palo Alto, CA**

- Before letting your children pour liquids from a pitcher, have them practice pouring dry items, such as rice or salt.

- Instead of giving children handfuls of eating utensils to pass out at snack time, let them use trays. Line the trays with sheets of colorful tissue paper and lay out the spoons, forks and napkins on top. The children will find the trays easy to hold when going around the table.

  Paulette M. Skinner, Reading, PA

- Let your children use muffin tins as trays when passing out cups of milk or juice. The muffin tins will help keep the cups from tipping over.

- To prevent accidental spills at snack time, encourage your children to put their cups or glasses above their plates toward the center of the table, rather than to the side.

  Cathryn Abraham, St. Charles, IL

Food tips

- When making pumpkin bread or other quick breads for snacks, double the recipe and bake half of the batter in a loaf pan and the other half in small metal juice cans. The large loaf can be eaten at snack time, and the miniature loaves can be taken home by the children as gifts.

  Karen Seehusen, Ft. Dodge, IA

- When making molded gelatin shapes for special occasions, add a teaspoon of white vinegar to the gelatin and water mixture. The shapes will hold up better when you take them out of the molds.

- Frozen snacks on sticks are a real favorite, but they're messy to eat. To catch drips, poke the sticks through the centers of small paper plates.

- Use ice cream cones for fun — and edible — snack containers.

- Cut egg cartons with lids in half the short way to make lunch boxes for snacks. Put small pieces of different foods in the egg cups. Your children will love having their snacks served this way!

- For holiday snacks, use cookies cutters to cut bread into holiday shapes and make them into sandwiches.

- Children really enjoy frosting their own cookies or muffins. To make the job easier and more fun, put the frosting into empty mustard or catsup squeeze bottles for them to use.

Learning through snacks

- Plan snacks that tie in with concepts your children are learning. For example, serve round crackers to review the circle shape. Or serve cucumber slices, celery sticks and lime juice and use green napkins and placemats to review the color green. Review numbers by having the children count how many pieces of food they will eat for their snacks.

    Yosie Yoshimura, Gardena, CA

- Reinforce color concepts by adding a few drops of food coloring to milk served at snack time. This may also encourage children who don't like milk to drink it.

    Linnae Newman, Reading, PA

Snack-time manners

- To encourage children to sit close to the table when eating, try using this saying: "Tummy to our table, girls and boys." The saying provides a clear picture of what the children are to do, and they are sure to use it as a reminder among themselves at snack time.   **Bronwen Evans, Reading, PA**

- Parents often object when children overeat at snack time. To help the children remember how much food is enough, try this saying: "One mouth, one glass of juice; two hands, two crackers." The children will enjoy repeating this saying to jog their own memories.   **Dr. Susan A. Miller, Kutztown, PA**

GROUP TIMES

Game tips

- To determine how long "fair turns" should last, use an hourglass egg timer. When the children learn how to use the timer themselves, you won't constantly be called upon to say when a turn is up. **Cathryn Abraham, St. Charles, IL**

- To make sure that each child gets a turn to start a game, perform a special job or be a leader, make name cards for all the children and put the cards in a box. Every time a child is needed for a task, pull a name card from the box, then put the card in a can. After every child has had a turn, put the name cards back in the box. The children will wait patiently, knowing that eventually everyone will get a turn.

  Peggy Wolf, Pittsburgh, PA

- Before playing games or relays, avoid the mix-up that can occur when children forget their team numbers by giving each child a wristband made of black or white elastic. This will help the "Black Bands" and the "White Bands" take their places quickly, and no time will be lost.

  Peggy Wolf, Pittsburgh, PA

- If you have a child who dislikes being blindfolded for games, let the child wear a stocking cap and pull it down over his or her eyes. Wearing the cap will help the child feel more in control.

Circle-time tips

- Sometime during the day, have your children join you in a close circle for "Special Talk Time" during which you discuss such things as manners or new behavior ideas. Your children will respond well to this intimate time, and you'll find that it's very effective. **Mrs. Leslie Wagner, Chadron, NE**

- A really nice way to end the week is to schedule a time for "Put-Ups." Let each child volunteer to say something nice about another classmate, such as thanking him or her for being a good friend, for sharing a toy or game, for helping with a task or for anything positive. Not only will "Put-Ups" make everyone feel good, they will also encourage more positive behavior. **Maxine Pincott, Windsor, CT**

- To help your children with name recognition, sit in a circle and place a small blanket loosely over a child's head. Then sing, "Who, oh, who, is under the blanket?" to the tune of "Ten Little Indians." After singing the first three lines, stop and let the other children in the circle name the child who is under the blanket. Continue around the circle until every child has had a turn. **Nancy Hartman, Fleetwood, PA**

Seating mats

- Make seating mats for your children to use at group time by writing their names on pizza wheels. Then let the children decorate their mats with felt markers. Not only will the mats help with name recognition, they'll also allow you to seat the children where you wish. **Debbie Scofield, Niceville, FL**

- Place large, colorful paper circles on the floor for the children to sit on during group time. When you collect the circles, use them to reinforce color recognition.
  Judy Laureano, Reading, PA

- To prevent arguments about who sits where at circle time, provide the children with personalized seating mats. For each child, cut out two 11"x12" sheets of vinyl wallpaper and punch holes about 1 inch apart around the edges. Place a magazine or a folded newspaper between the wallpaper sheets to make a "cushion." Then let the child use yarn to lace the sheets together. Write the children's names on the finished mats and place them on the floor before circle time begins. You'll find that the mats will also help with name recognition.
  Jackie Stevison, St. Louis, MO

Carpet seating

- Do your children tend to "bunch up" on the floor at group time? They'll give each other more space if you make a big square on the carpet with masking tape for them to sit on.

  Kathy Rogaway, Palo Alto, CA

Sharing tips

- For sharing times, make a drawstring bag and write "Show and Tell" and your school's name on it with a felt marker. When it's a child's turn to share, let him or her take the bag home and bring back something that fits in the bag for Show and Tell.

  Melissa Keck, Oswego, IL

- Sharing time will go smoother if you limit the number of children who share each day. Listeners will be more attentive and polite. And the children will take great care in deciding what to bring for sharing on their own special day.

  Nancy C. Windes, Denver, CO

- Here's a way to schedule your Show and Tell times. Divide your class into five groups and assign one day of the week to each group as its sharing day. For each group, make a Sharing Day chart that includes the name of the day and the names of the children. Use a different color of paper and matching ink for each chart and cover the finished charts with clear Con-Tact paper. When the charts are displayed on the appropriate days, they will remind the children of special sharing times as well as aid in color and name recognition.

  Nancy C. Windes, Denver, CO

- Provide a corner or table in the room for displaying items brought in for sharing. Have a special time for the children to go by the corner or table to see what's on display and to listen to those who have something to share.

  Betty Ruth Baker, Waco, TX

Behavior tips

- Outdoor "treasure hunts" are a good way to help children run off excess energy. Easter egg hunts are always fun in spring. And in the fall, your children will enjoy searching for pumpkins which they can bring inside and decorate during art time.
  Mrs. Leslie Wagner, Chadron, NE

- For a young child, tearing newspaper is an excellent way to release the tense energy buildup which often accompanies anger. As the paper is torn, the child can also be encouraged to yell. Afterwards, have the child help with the newspaper cleanup.
  Kathleen Tobey, Griffith, IN

- As a quieter alternative, let the child tear sheets of newspaper into many small pieces.
  Kathleen Tobey, Griffith, IN

- In times of stress, playing with shaving cream can have a calming effect on young children. Have them wear smocks or let them partially undress. Then spray the shaving cream on a table and let them use it to arm-paint or to rub on their bodies and heads. A little water is all it takes for easy cleanup.
  Kathleen Tobey, Griffith, IN

- Help your children release feelings of stress or anger by providing them with a special pillow to use as a punching bag.

- When children play with flying toys, such as airplanes and helicopters, they sometimes get carried away and start running around the room. To prevent this, make a rule that the children must either be seated or standing on their knees when playing with such toys.
  Debbie Scofield, Niceville, FL

CLEANUP TIMES

Toy containers

- Cleanup time will be easier if you put identifying pictures on the outsides of toy containers.

  Cathryn Abraham, St. Charles, IL

- To make cleanup easier and play the next time more fun, make drawstring bags in several different colors and let the children use them for sorting and storing toys. The color of each bag — or a label on the outside — can indicate which toys should be put inside it. **Ellen Javernick, Loveland, CO**

Getting the job done

- Use a kitchen timer to encourage your children to clean up quickly between activities. Tell them how many minutes they have to work, then set the timer to go off when the time is up. At the sound of the bell, everyone should be finished and seated, ready for the next activity.

  Carol W. Adams, Clinton, MD

- As a gentle reminder to the children that it's time to clean up and come to the circle for group activities, turn on a music box. You will soon find many children trying to "beat Mr. Music" by joining the circle before the music box runs down.

  Sister Roberta Bailey, OSB, Dade City, FL

- Make cleanup time more fun by singing this song to the tune of "Frere Jacques":

  > Time to clean up, time to clean up
  > All the toys, all the toys.
  > Time to put the toys away.
  > Won't you please help me today?
  > Thank you. Thank you.

  Carol J. Luckenbill, Bernville, PA

TOTLINE
NEWSLETTER

24 pages full of ideas for working with preschool children.

Written by
Jean Warren

The **Totline** features activities for art, music, creative movement, coordination, language, science and self-awareness plus learning games, party ideas, sugarless snacks, original stories, feature articles and a special infant-toddler page.

Sample Issue $1.00   Price: $12 year (6 issues)

PRESCHOOL PATTERNS

Huge full-scale patterns to make your **Totline** come alive!

Three giant (22"x34") pattern sheets per issue.

Each Pattern packet is filled with:
- Flannelboard Patterns
- Room Decorations
- Large Arts & Crafts Patterns
- Actual Games — and Much More!

Price: $18 year — 6 packets per year to accompany your **Totline** newsletter.

TOTLINE PRESS
Piggyback Songs

- New songs sung to the tune of childhood favorites
- No music to read
- No tunes to forget
- Chorded for guitar or auto harp

Piggyback Songs, 64 pp. **$4.95**

More Piggyback Songs, 96 pp. **$6.95**

Piggyback Songs for Infants & Toddlers, 80 pp. .. **$6.95**

Super Snacks
by Jean Warren

Seasonal Sugarless Snacks
- No Honey • No Sugar
- No Artificial Sweeteners

160 Recipes   64 pp.

Price: $3.95

TOTLINE PRESS

1•2•3 ART

Over 200 art ideas compiled by Jean Warren

An open-ended collection of art ideas for working with young children. Over 200 activities that emphasize materials and process rather than specific end products. This is truly a "no-lose" art book for toddlers, preschool, kindergarten and special d students.

60 pp.   **Price: $12.95**

CUT & TELL STORIES

by Jean Warren

"Cut & Tell" Stories for Fall **$5.95**

"Cut & Tell" Stories for Winter **$5.95**

"Cut & Tell" Stories for Spring **$5.95**

ach book contains eight original stories plus directions for folding nd cutting a paper plate into a delightful story character.

OTHER BOOKS BY JEAN WARREN

Play & Learn Series

- Crafts $6.95
- Learning Games $6.95
- Language Games........... $6.95
- Story Time $6.95
- Science Time $6.95
- Movement Time............ $6.95

All materials available from:

**Totline Press
Warren Publishing House, Inc.
Box 2255
Everett, WA 98203**

Catalogs **FREE** upon request.